ENJOY COLORING!!

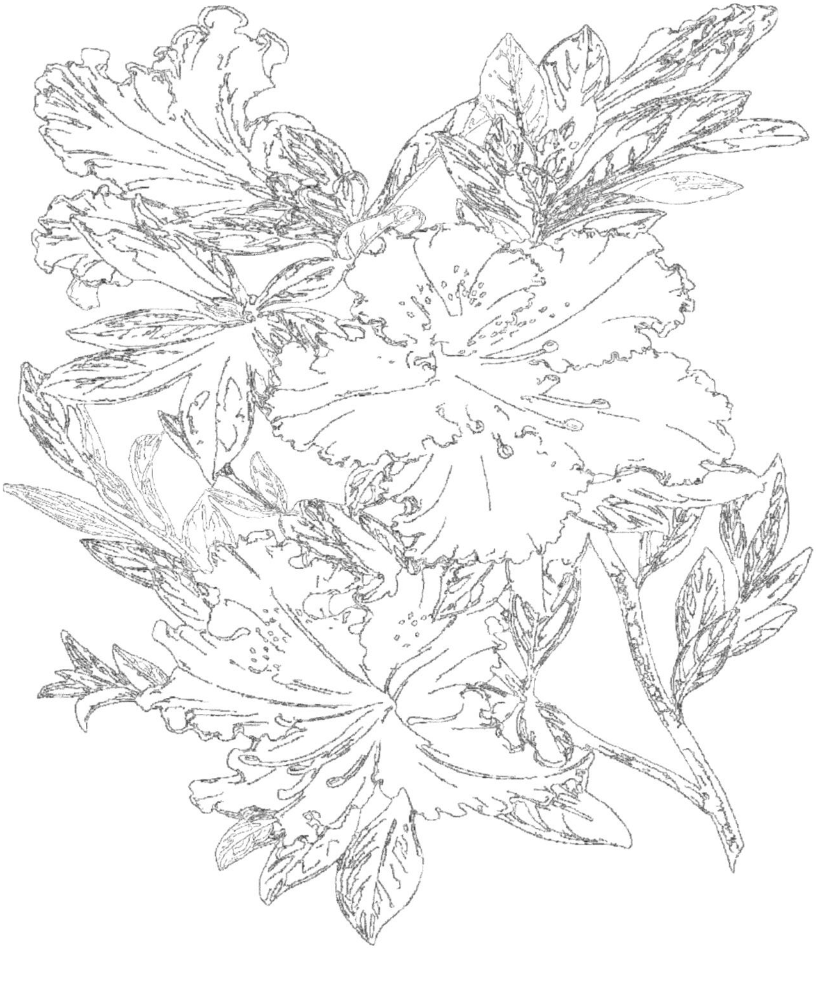

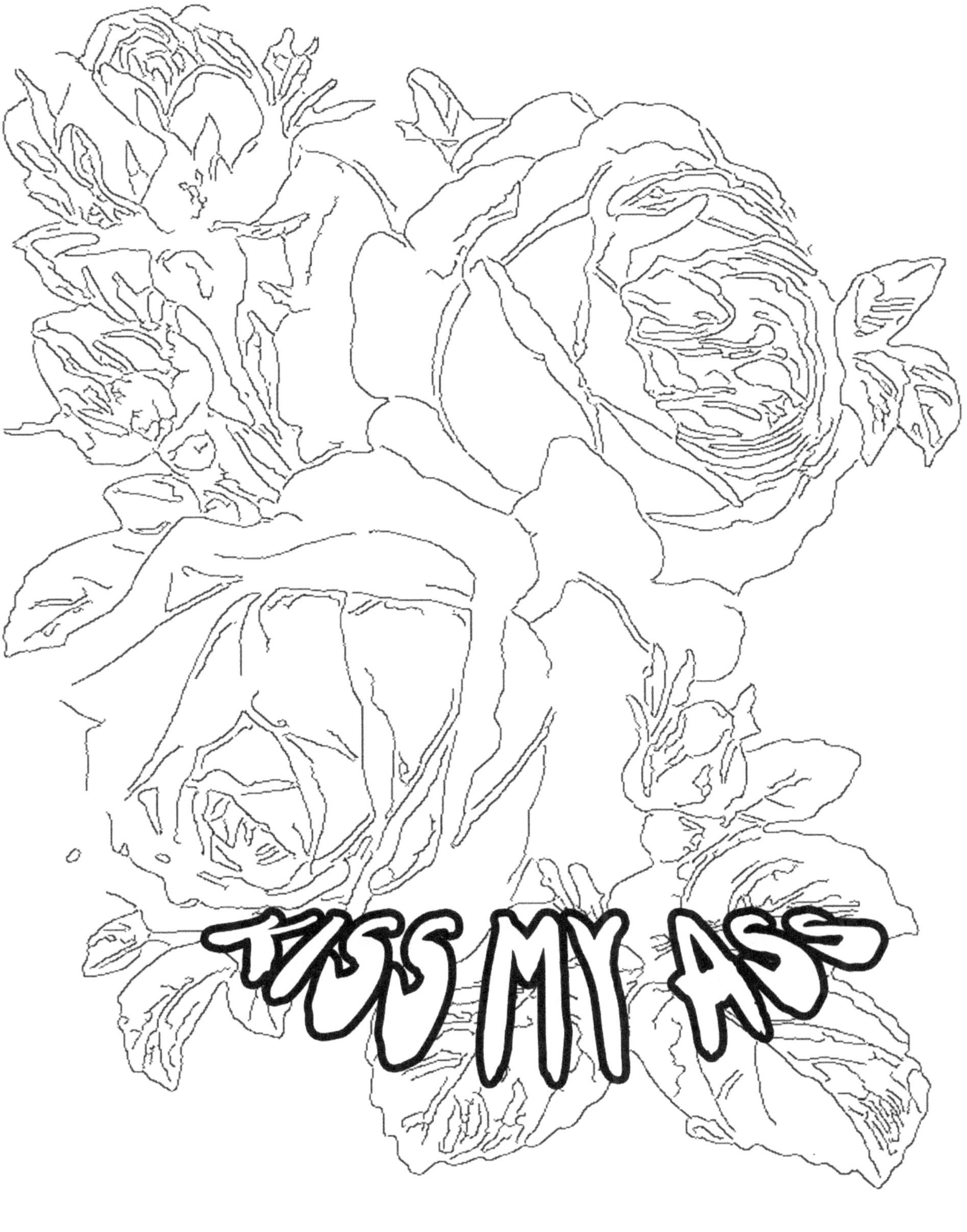
KISS MY ASS

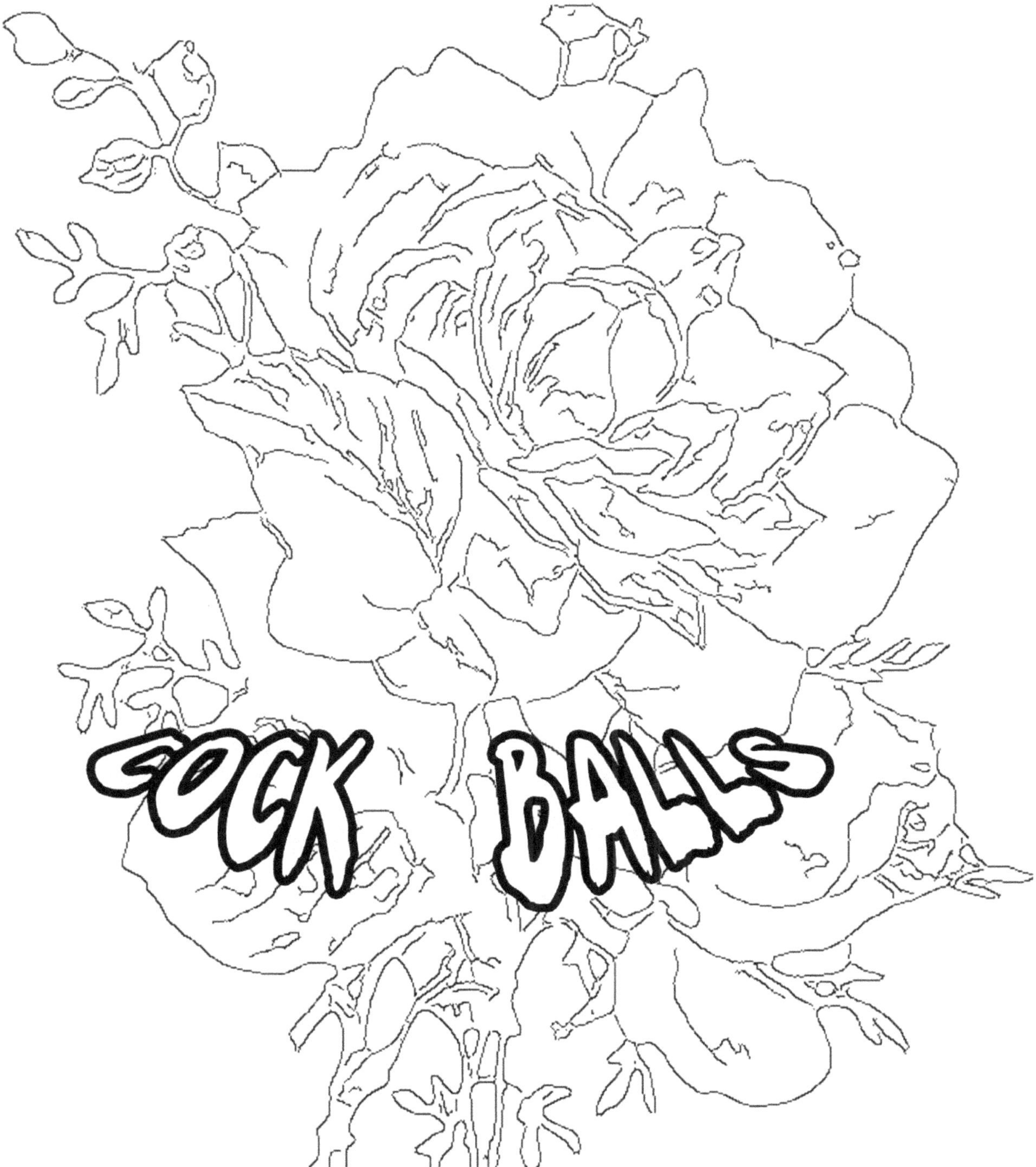
COCK BALLS

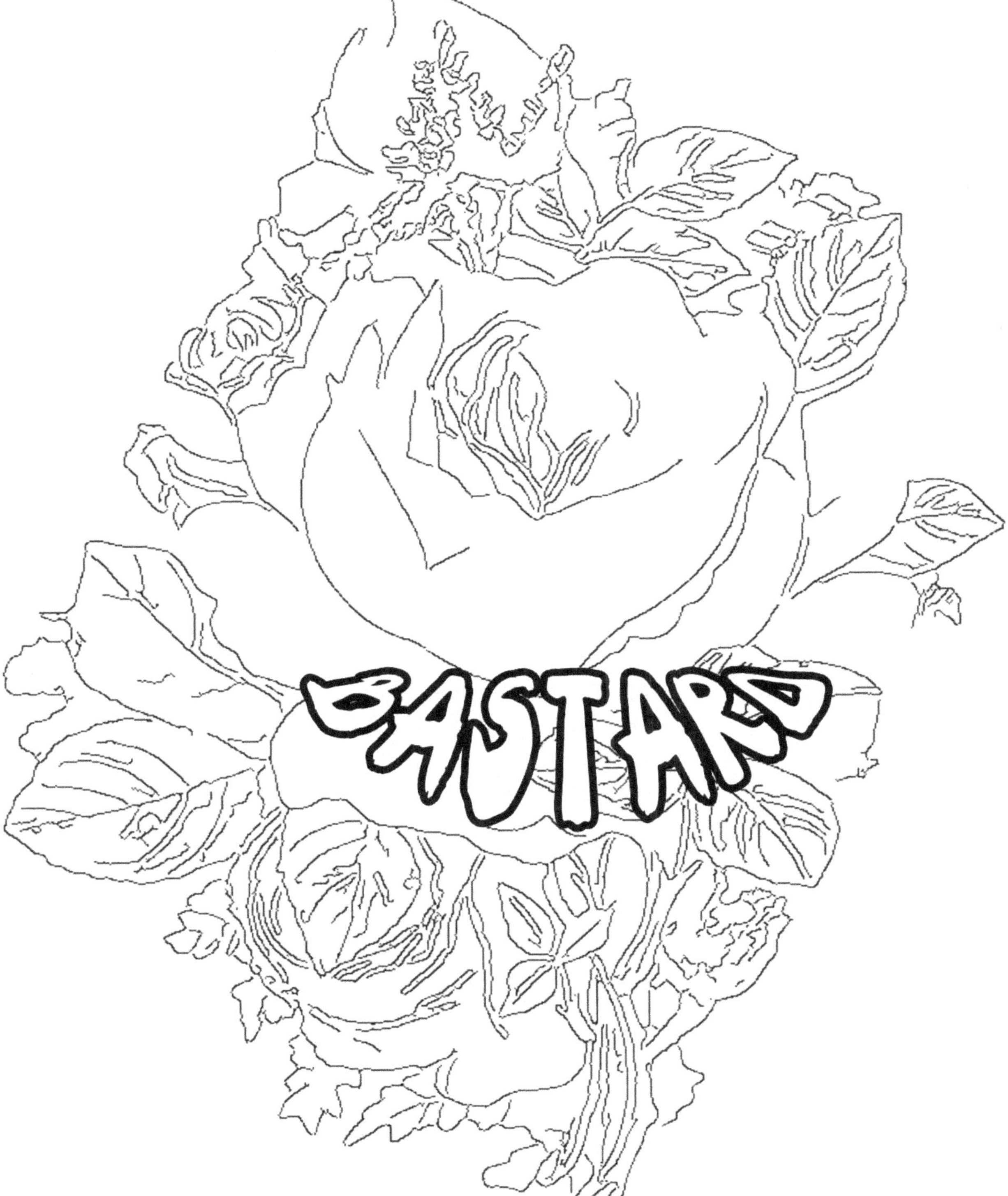
BASTARD

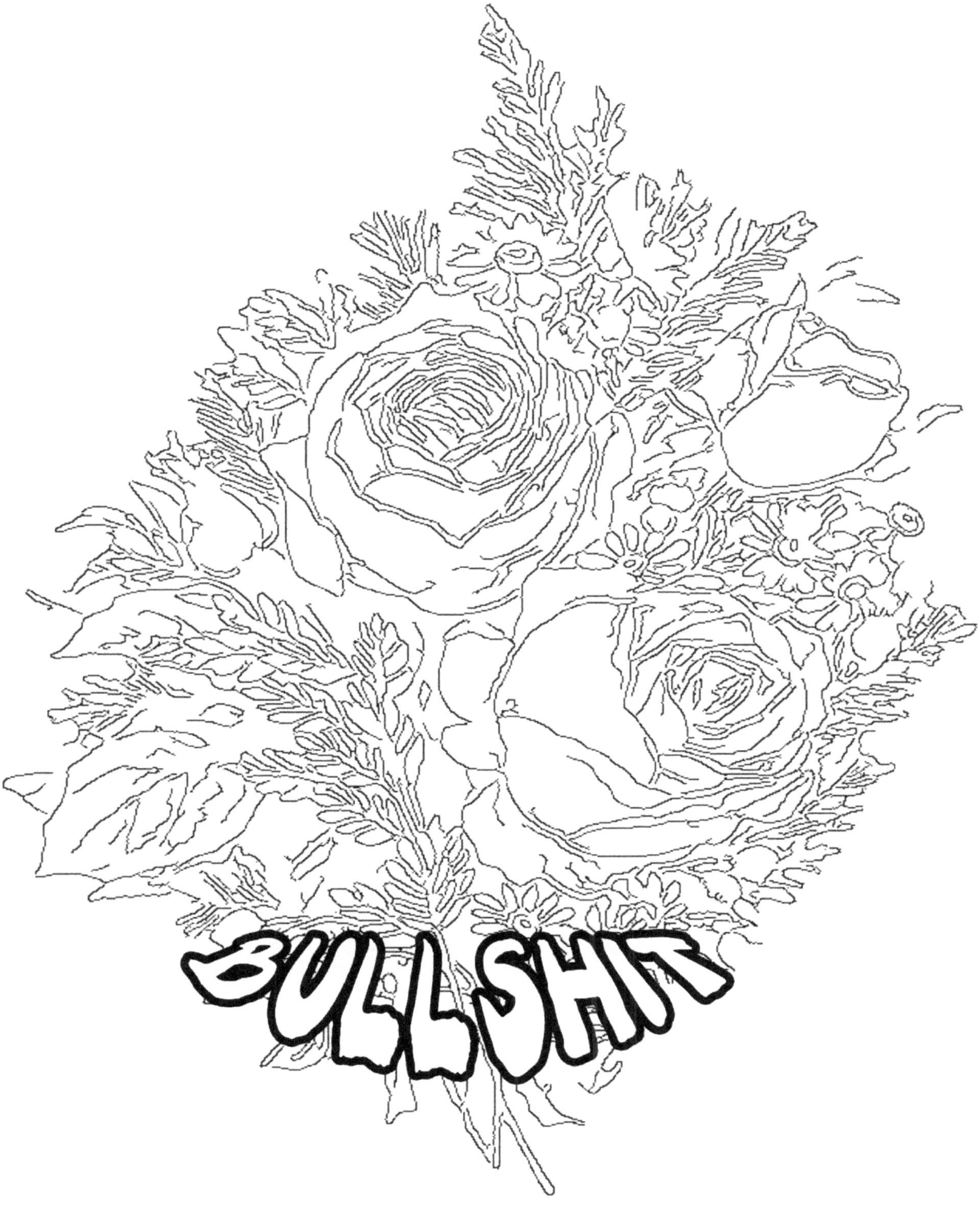
BULLSHIT

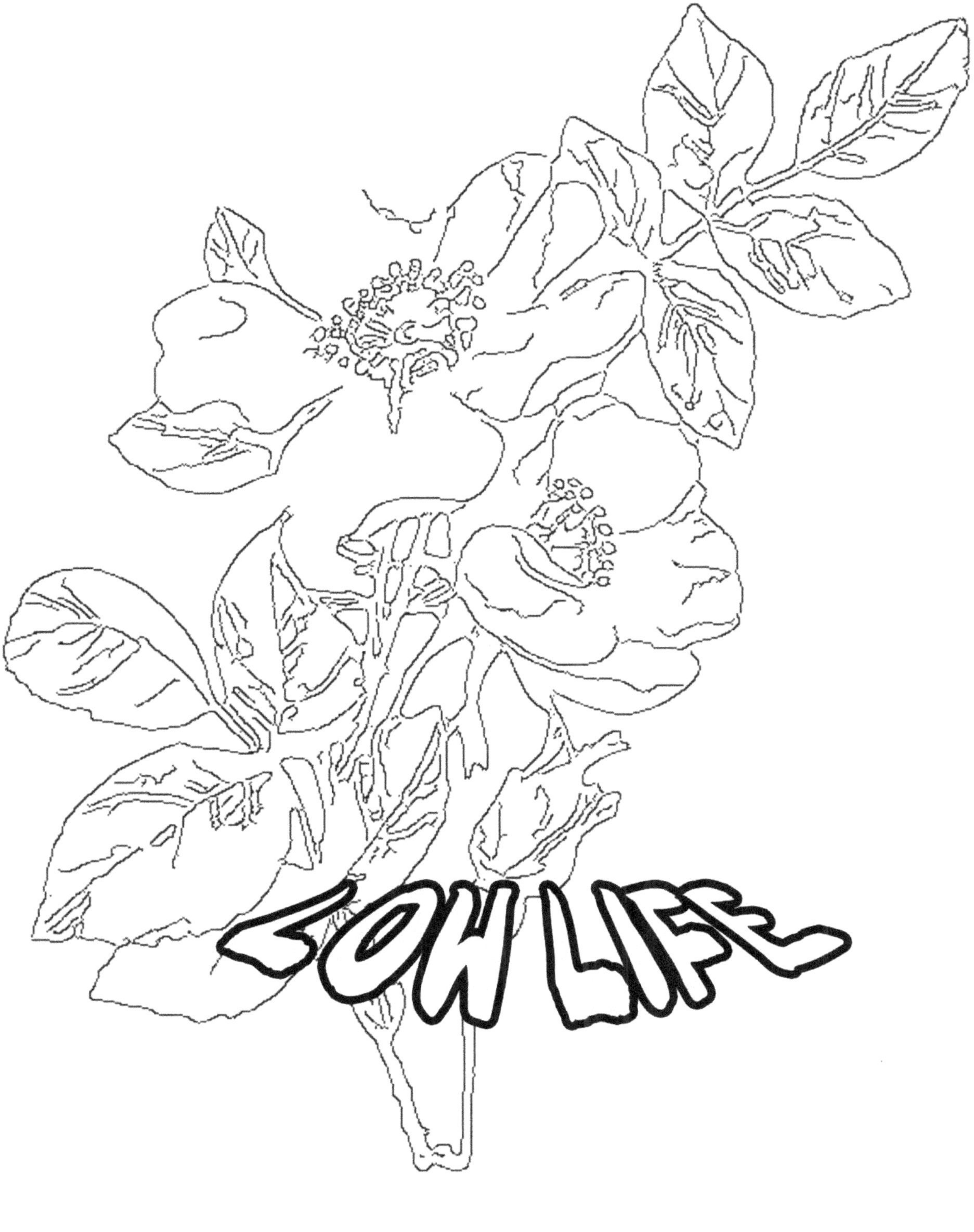
LOW LIFE

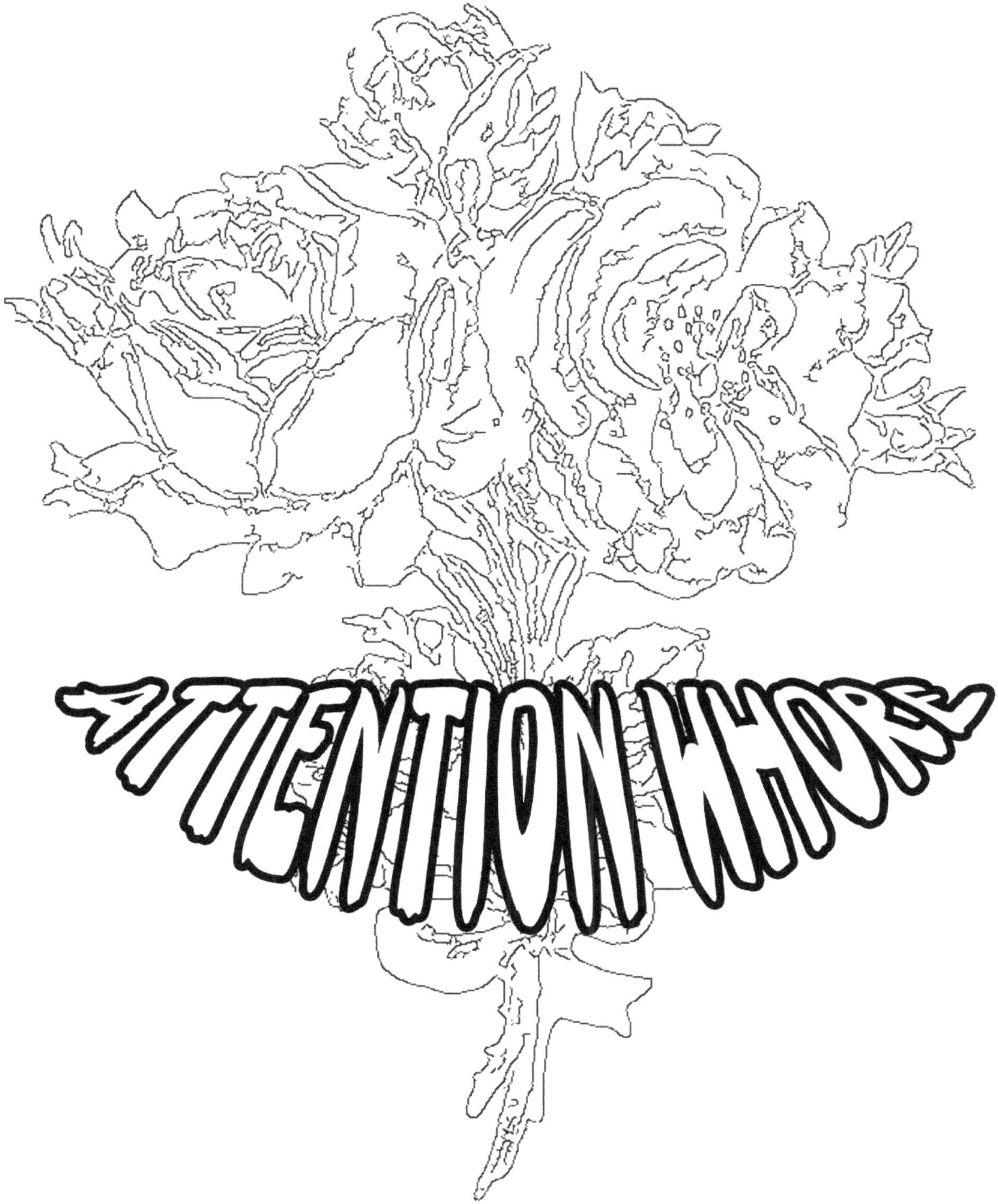
ATTENTION WHORE

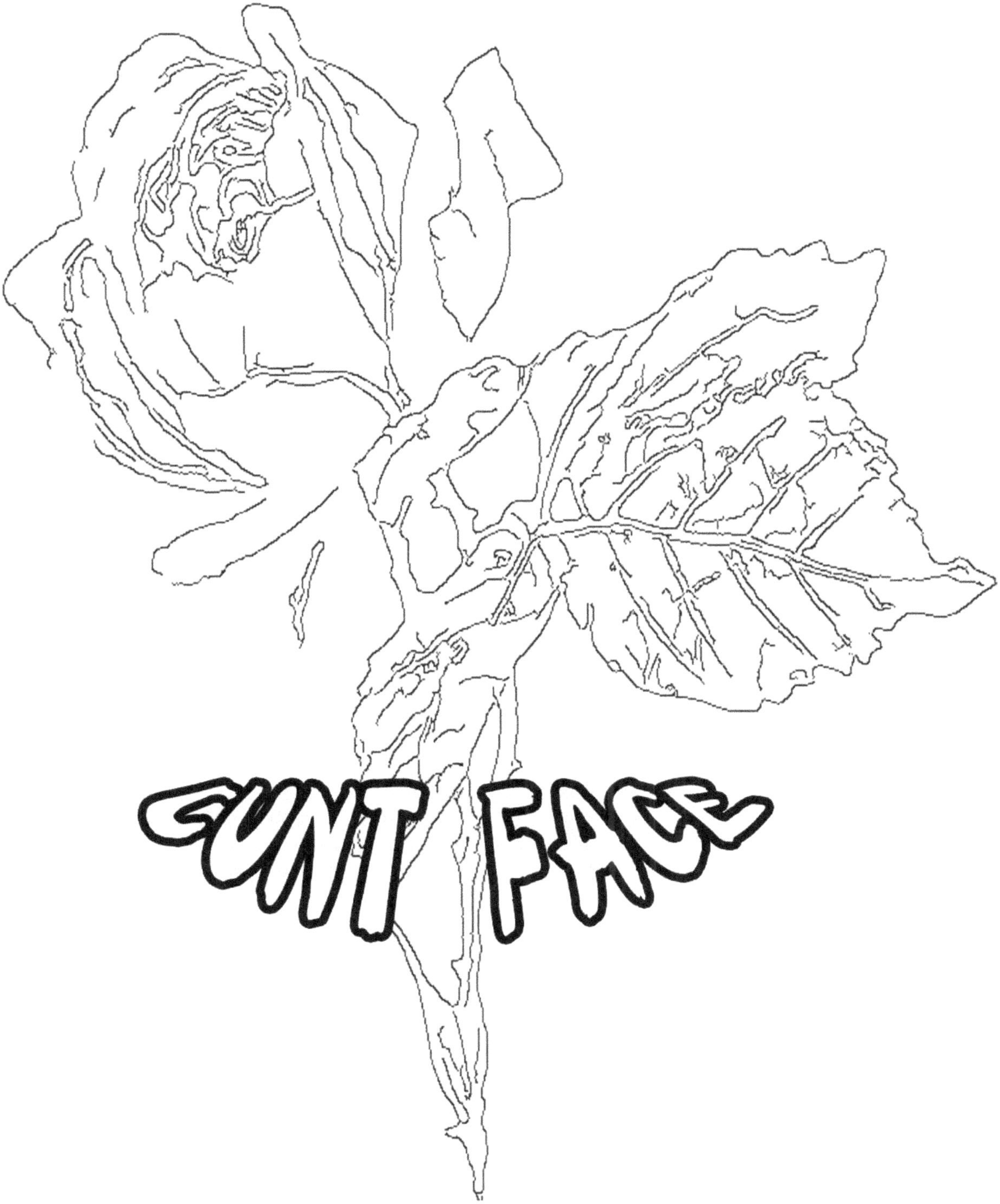
CUNT FACE

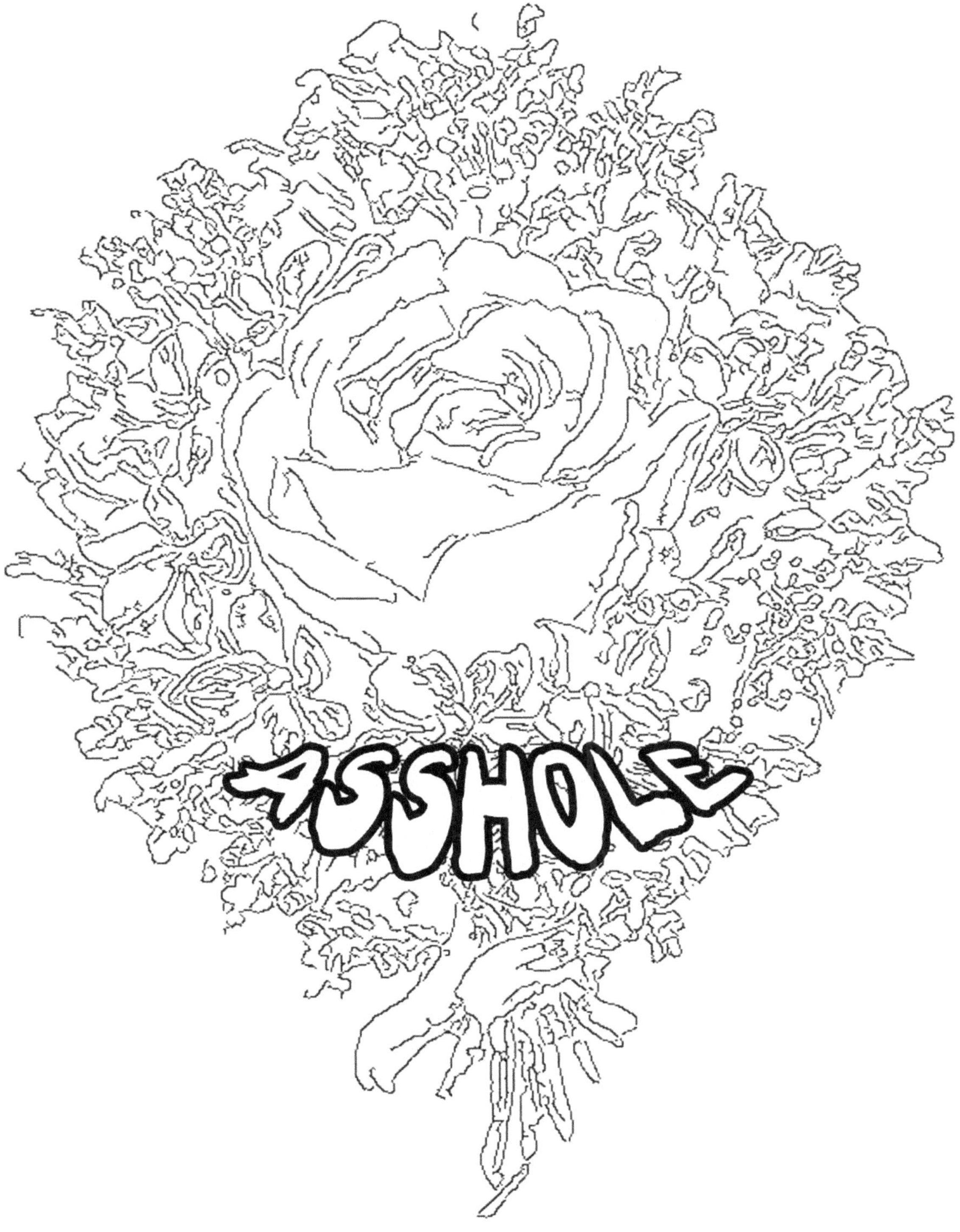
ASSHOLE

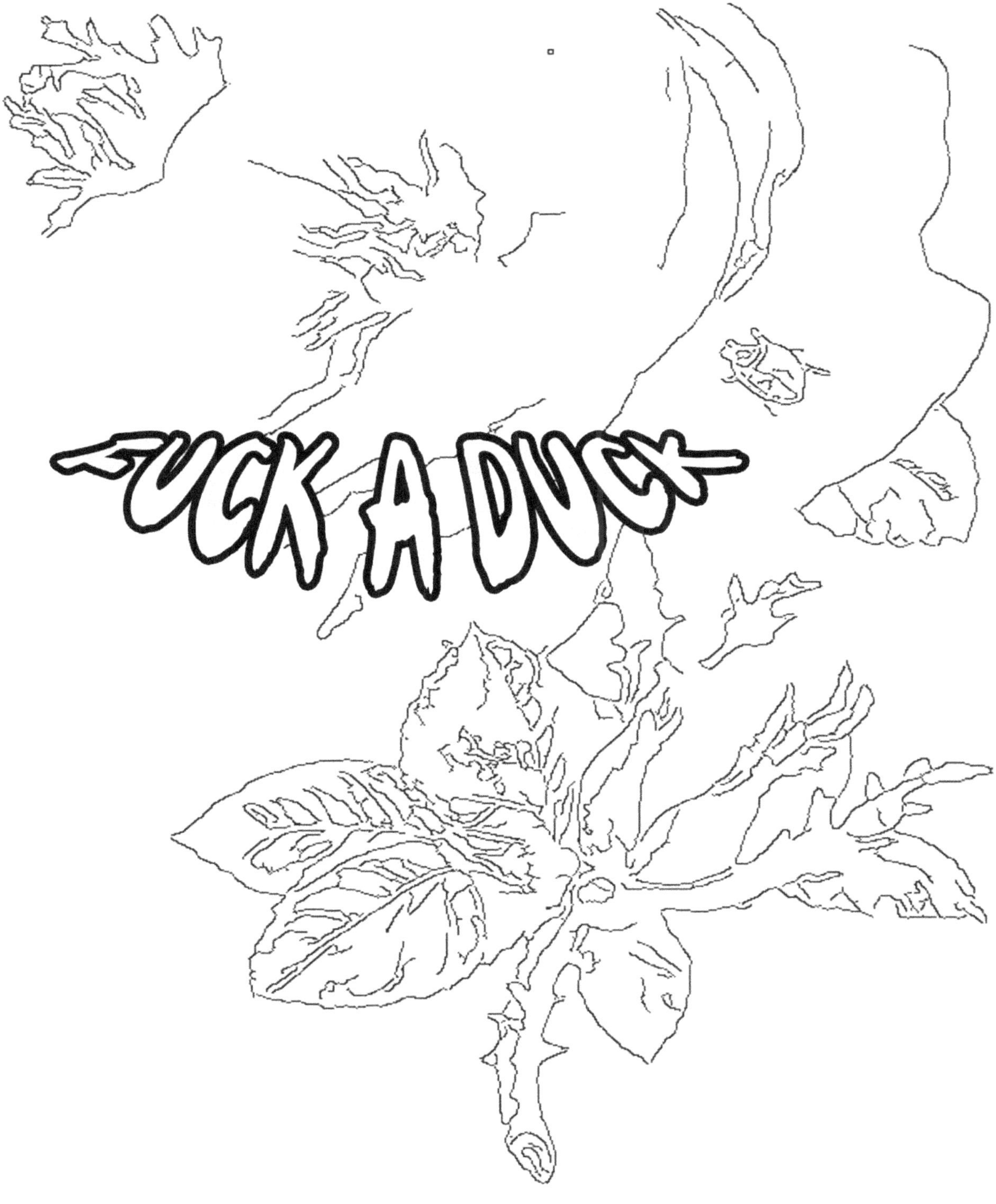
FUCK A DUCK

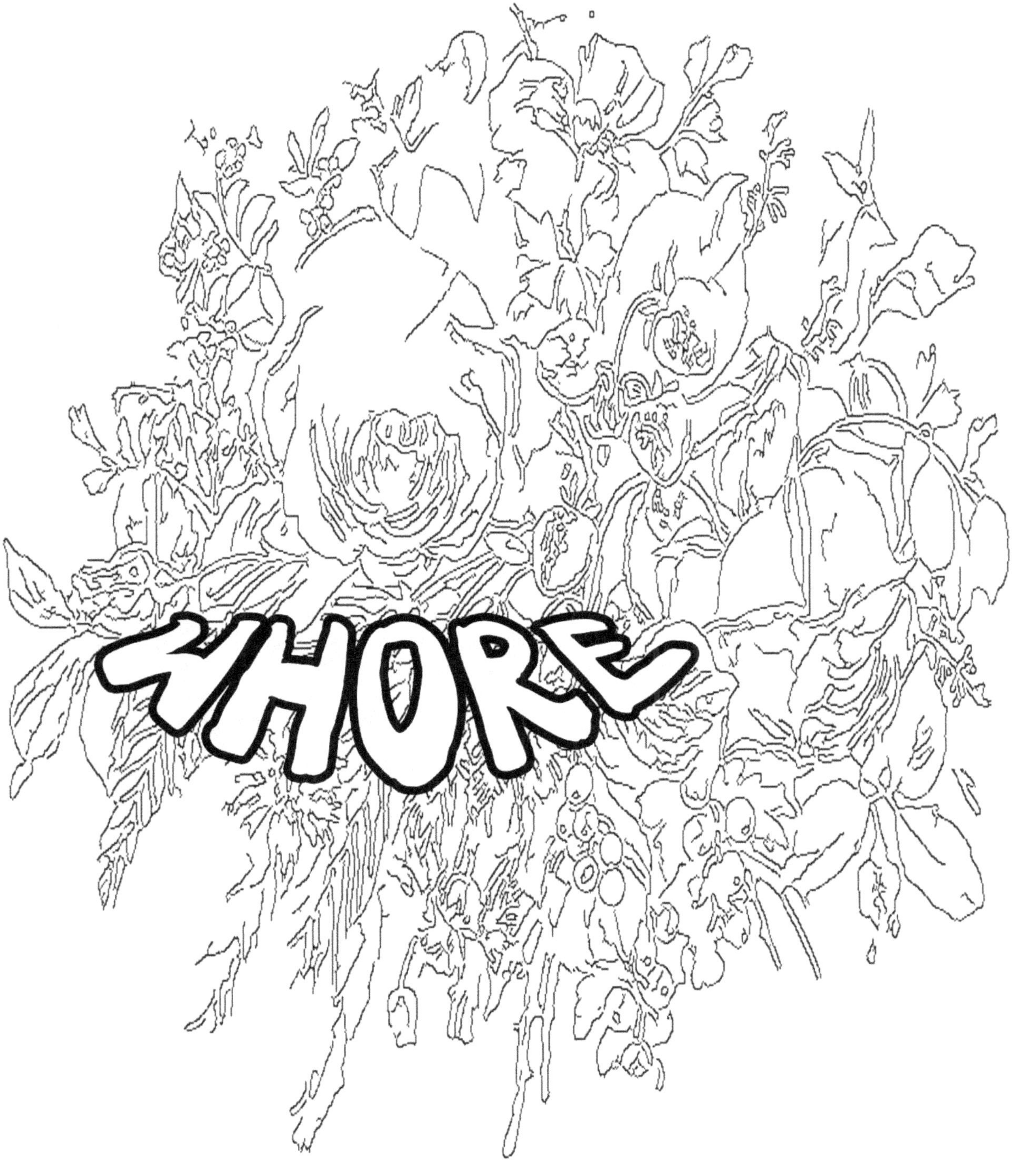
WHORE

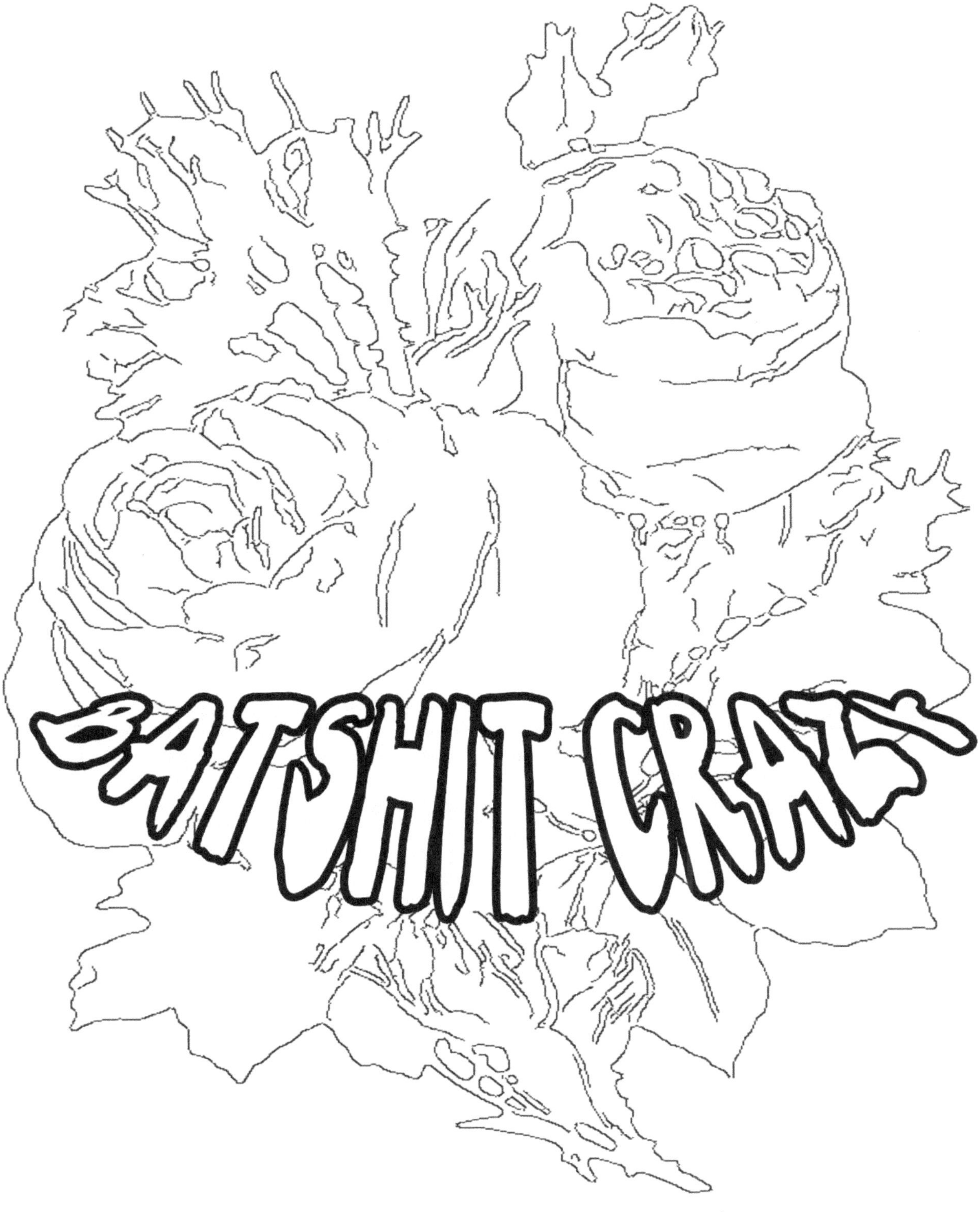
BATSHIT CRAZY

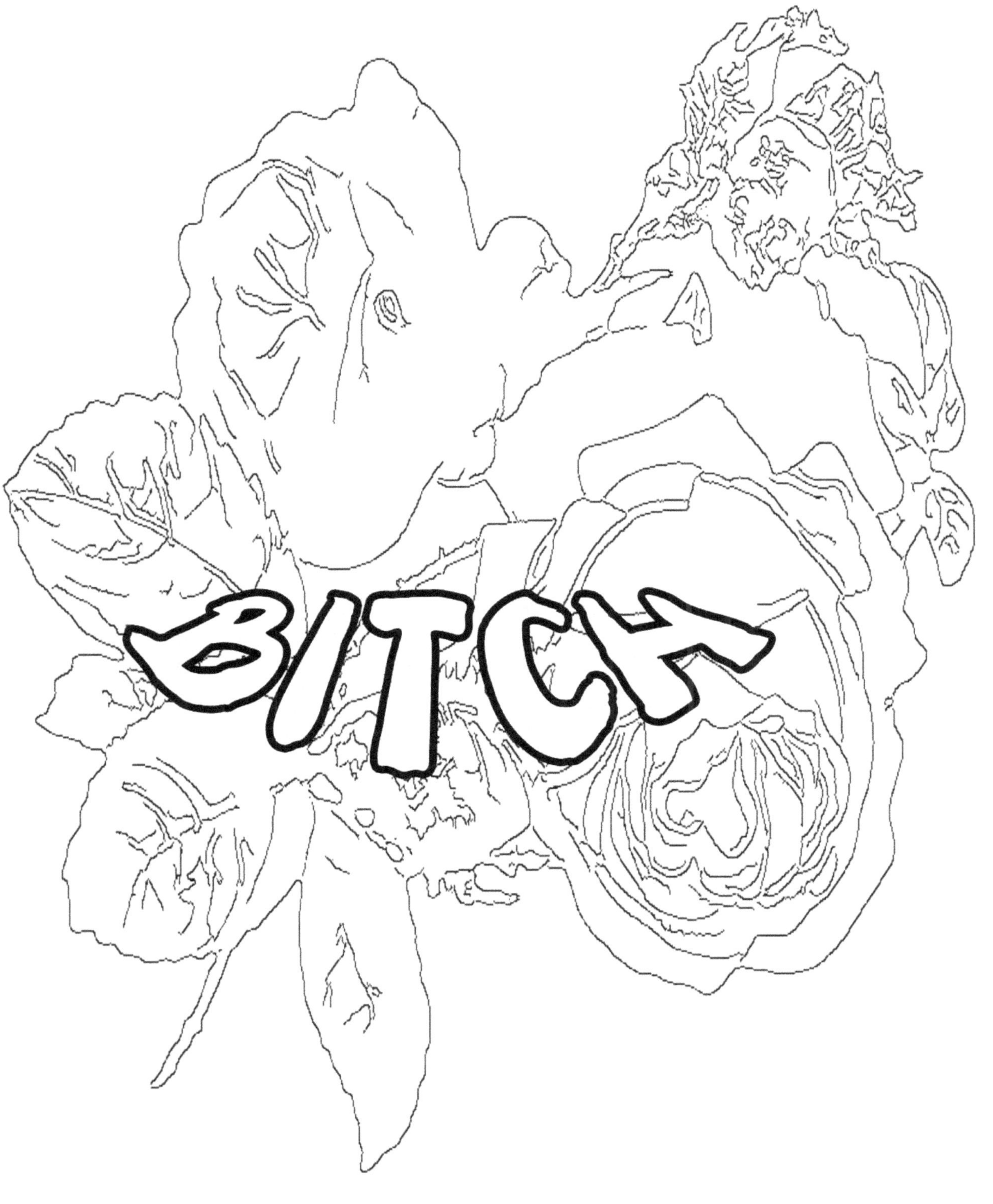
BITCH

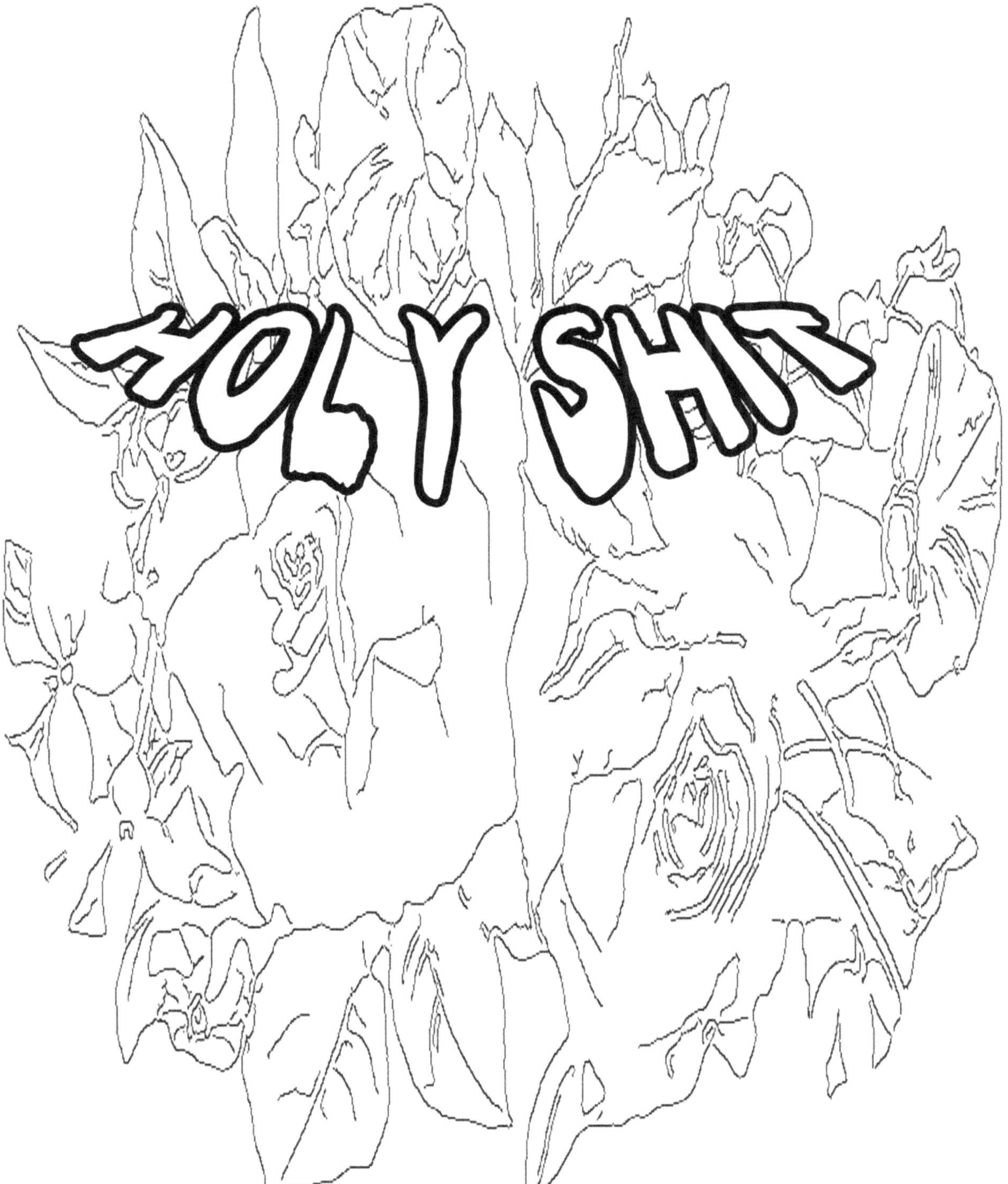
HOLY SHIT

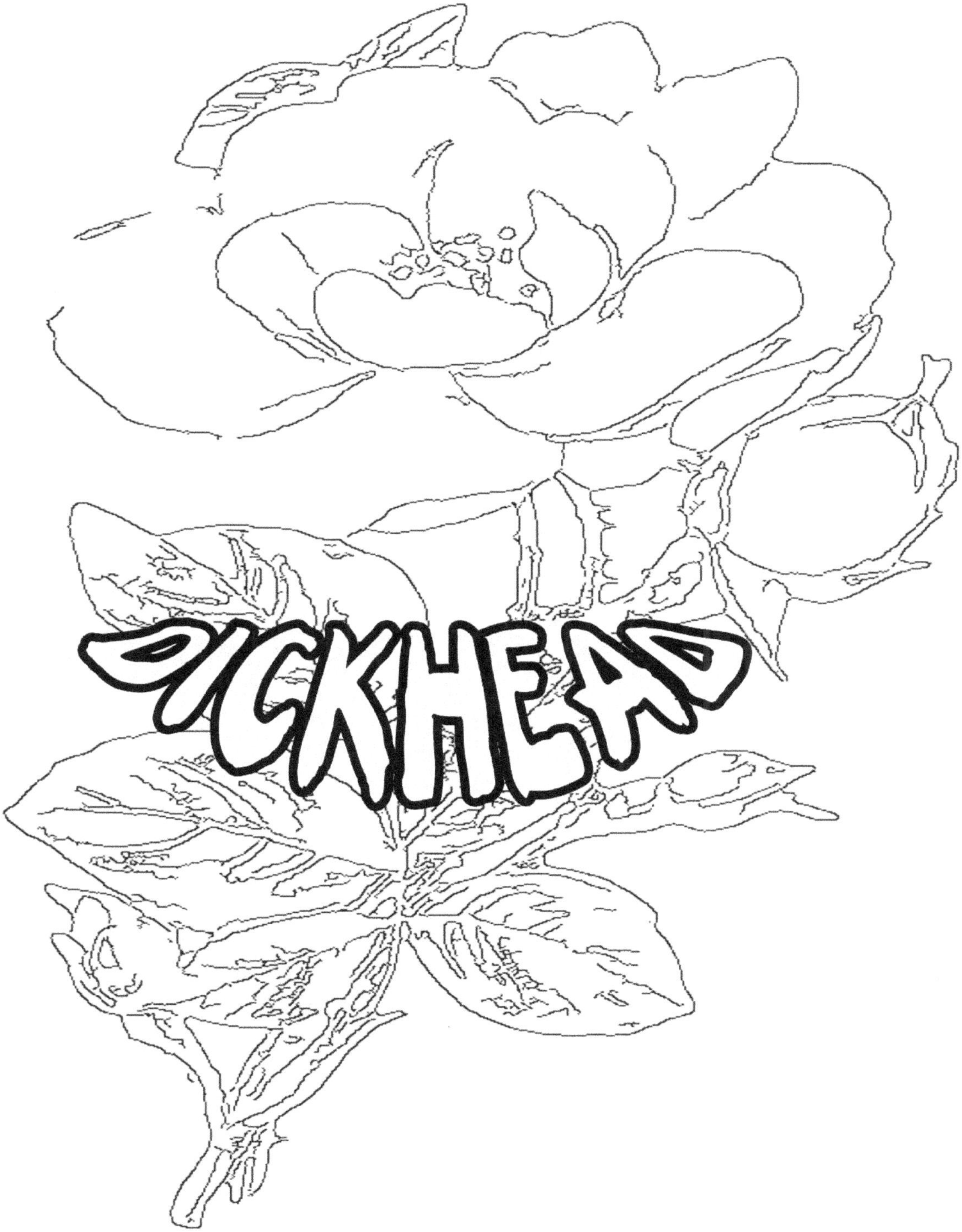
DICKHEAD

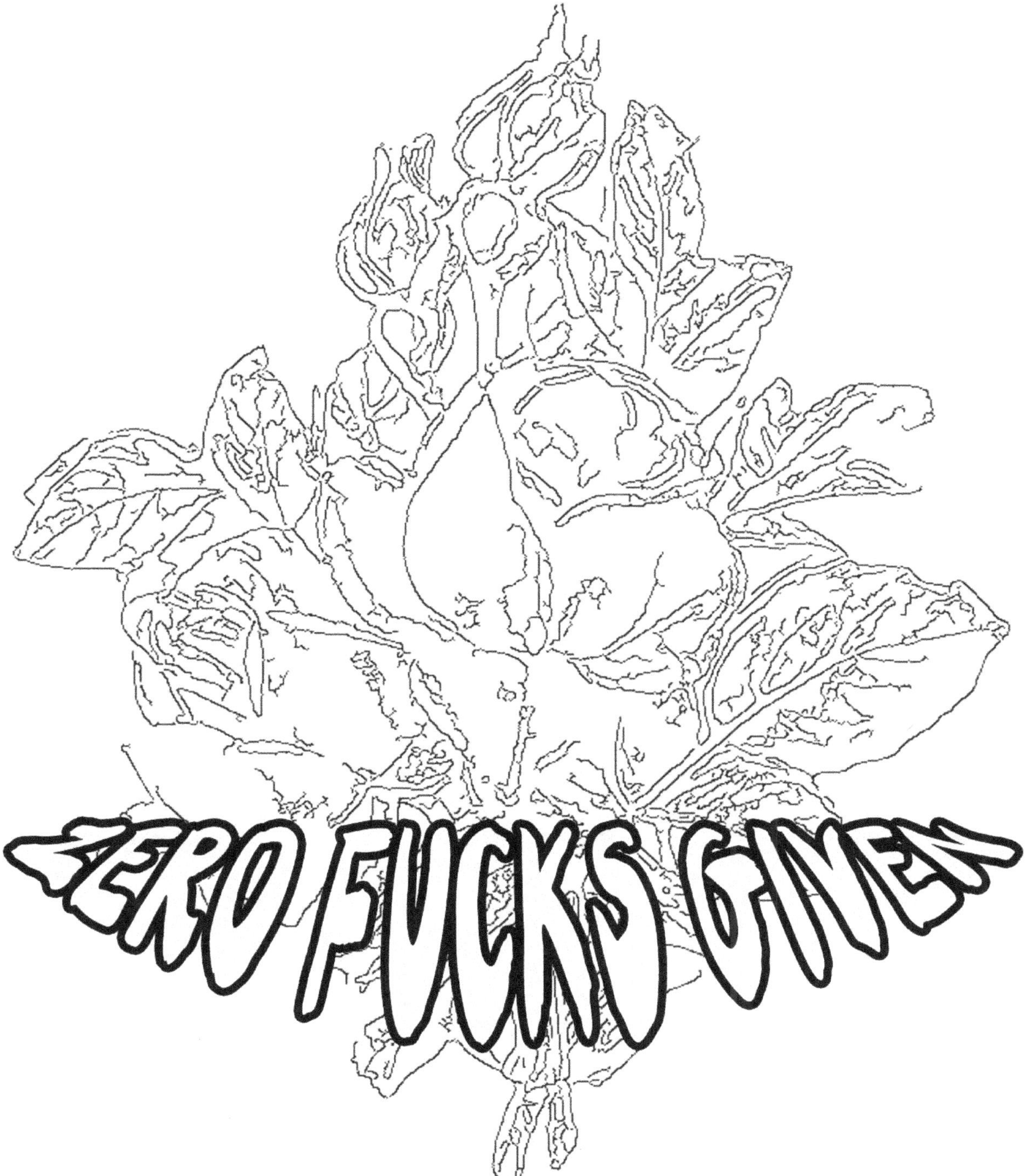
ZERO FUCKS GIVEN

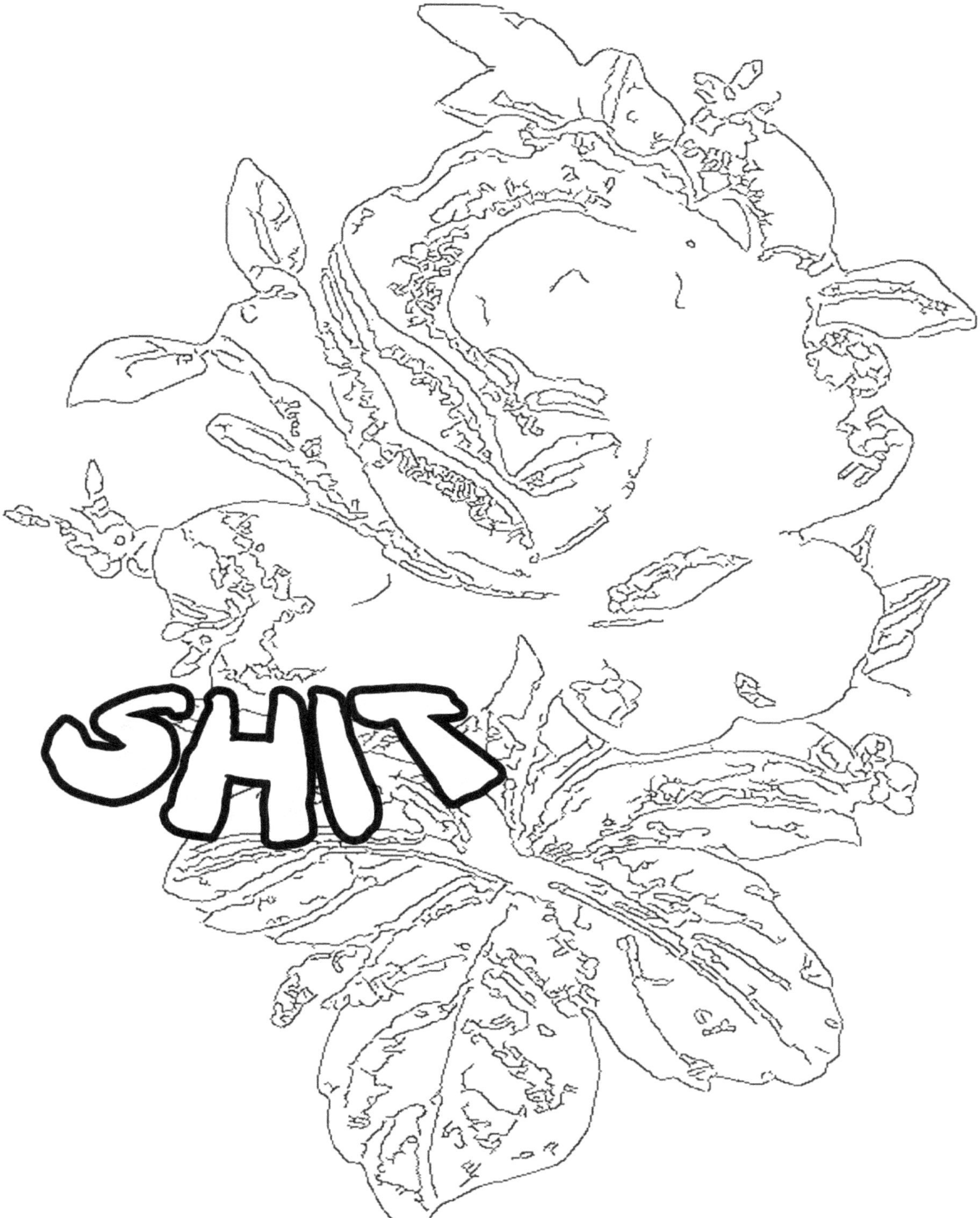
SHIT

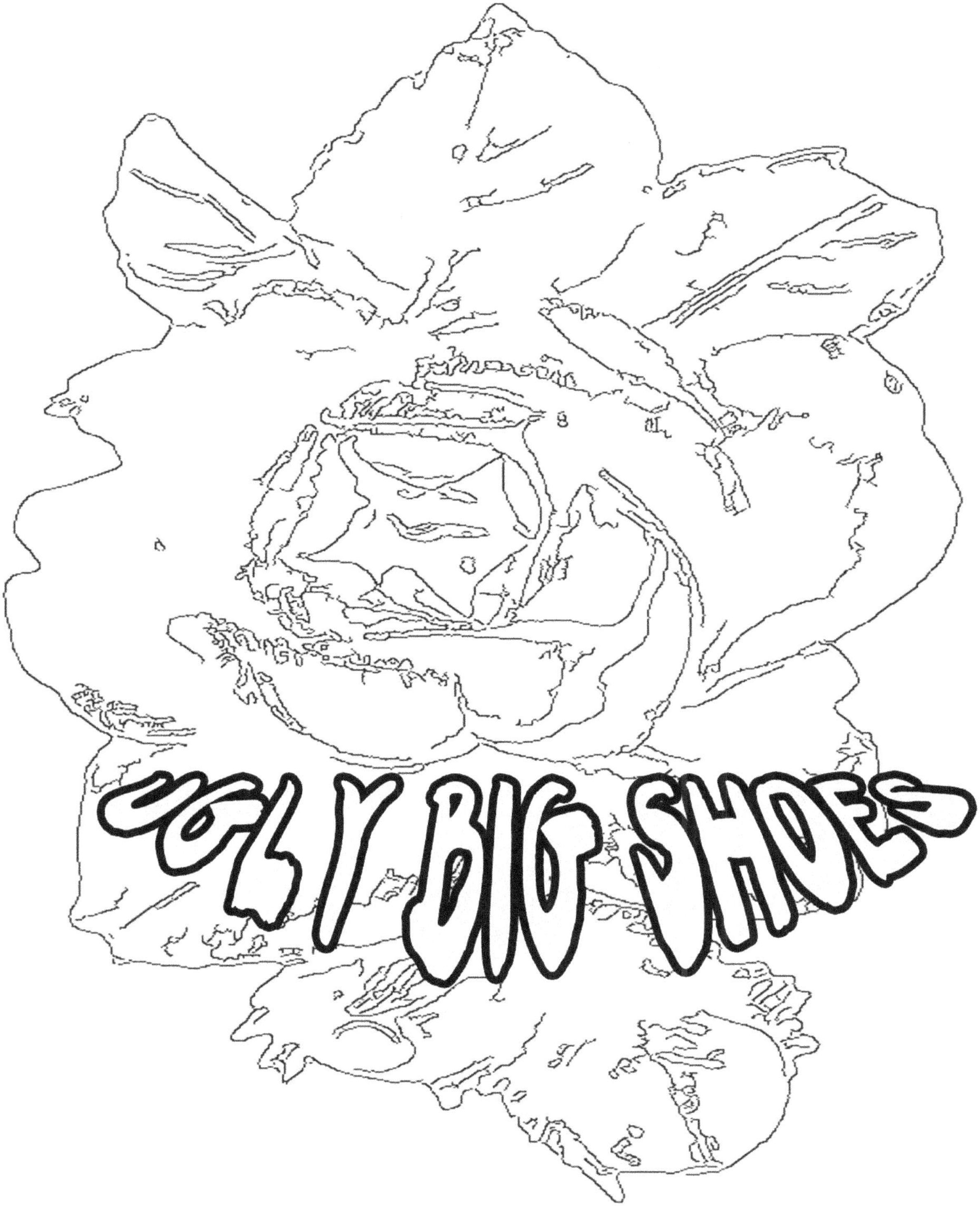
UGLY BIG SHOES

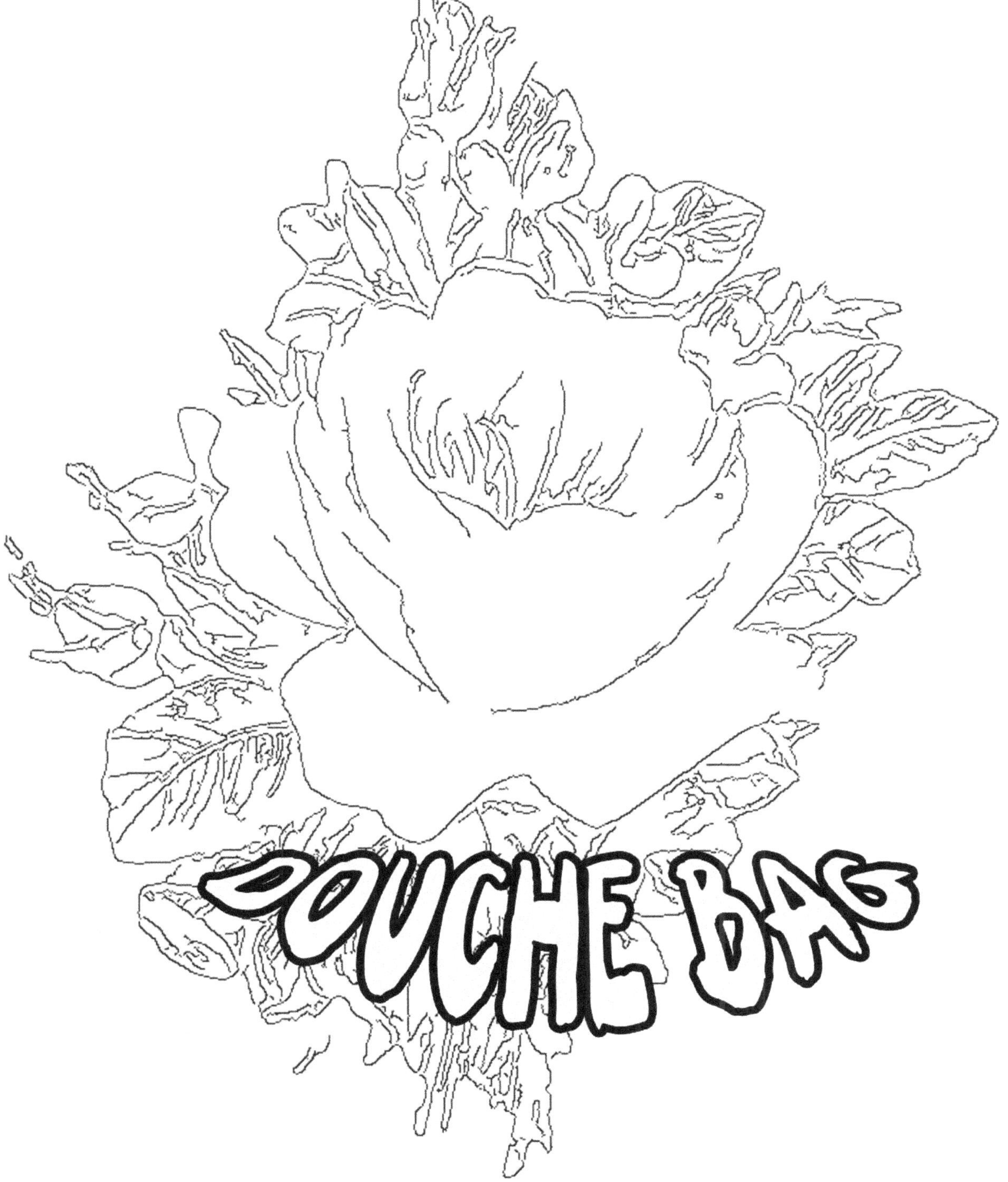
DOUCHE BAG

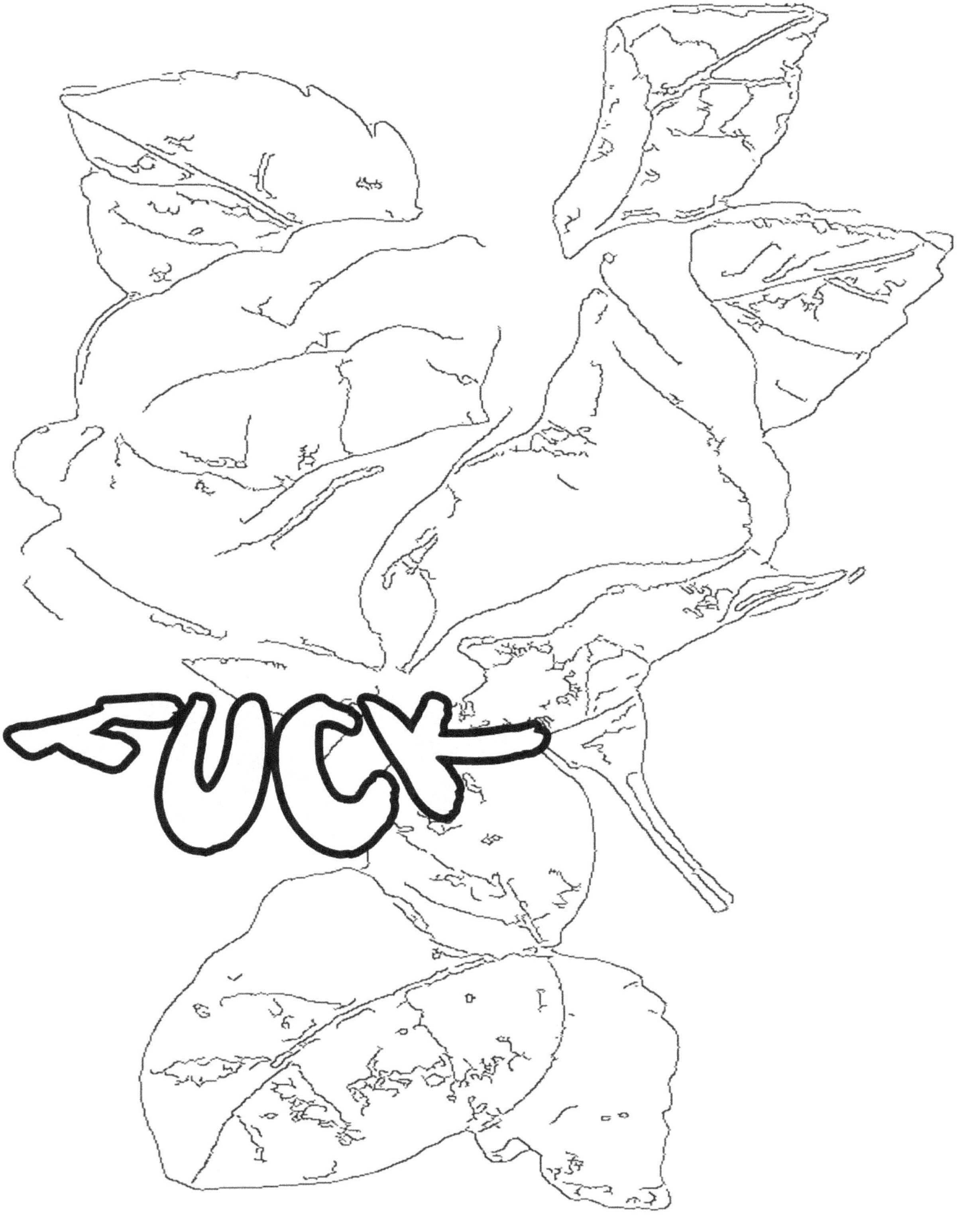
FUCK

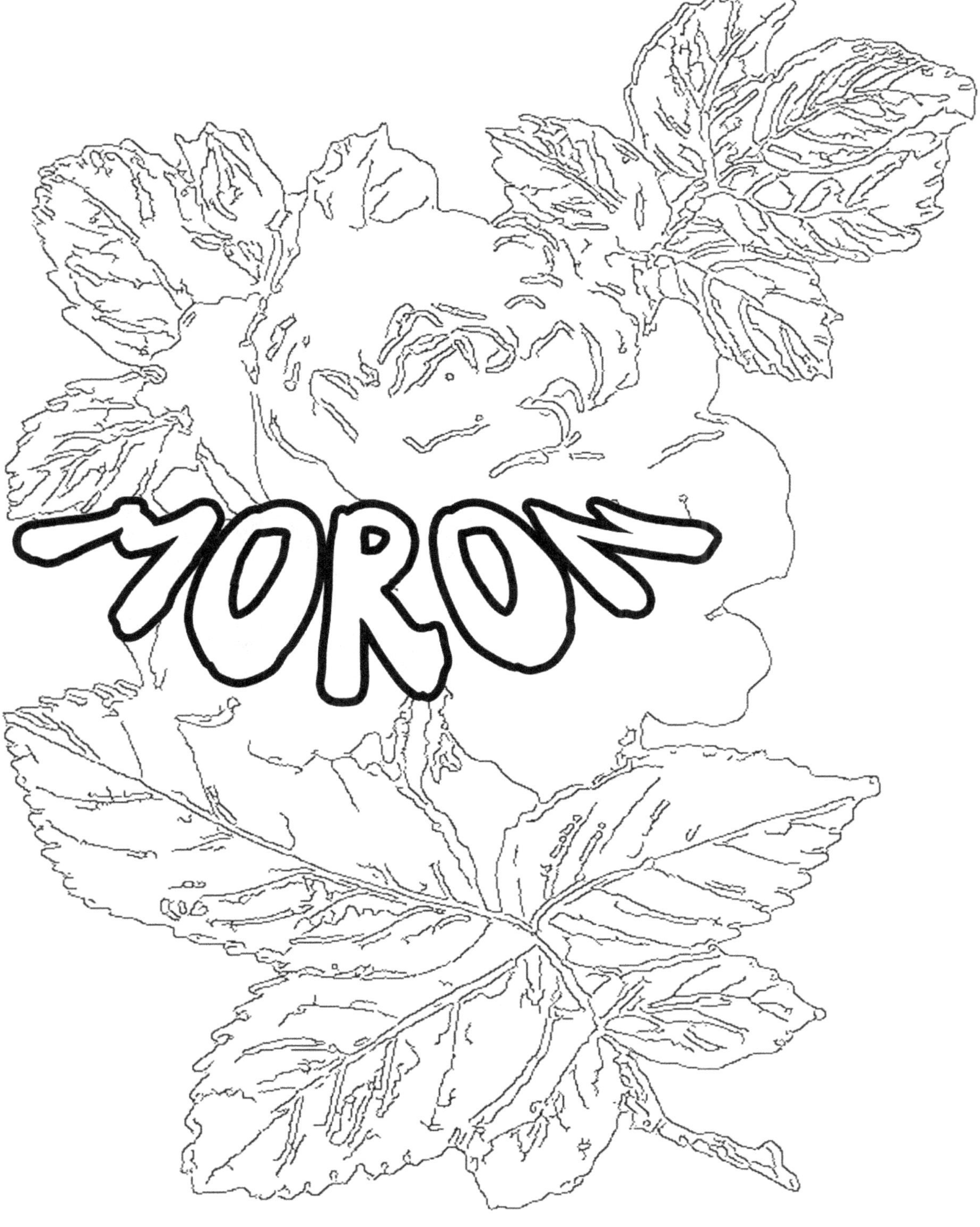
MORON

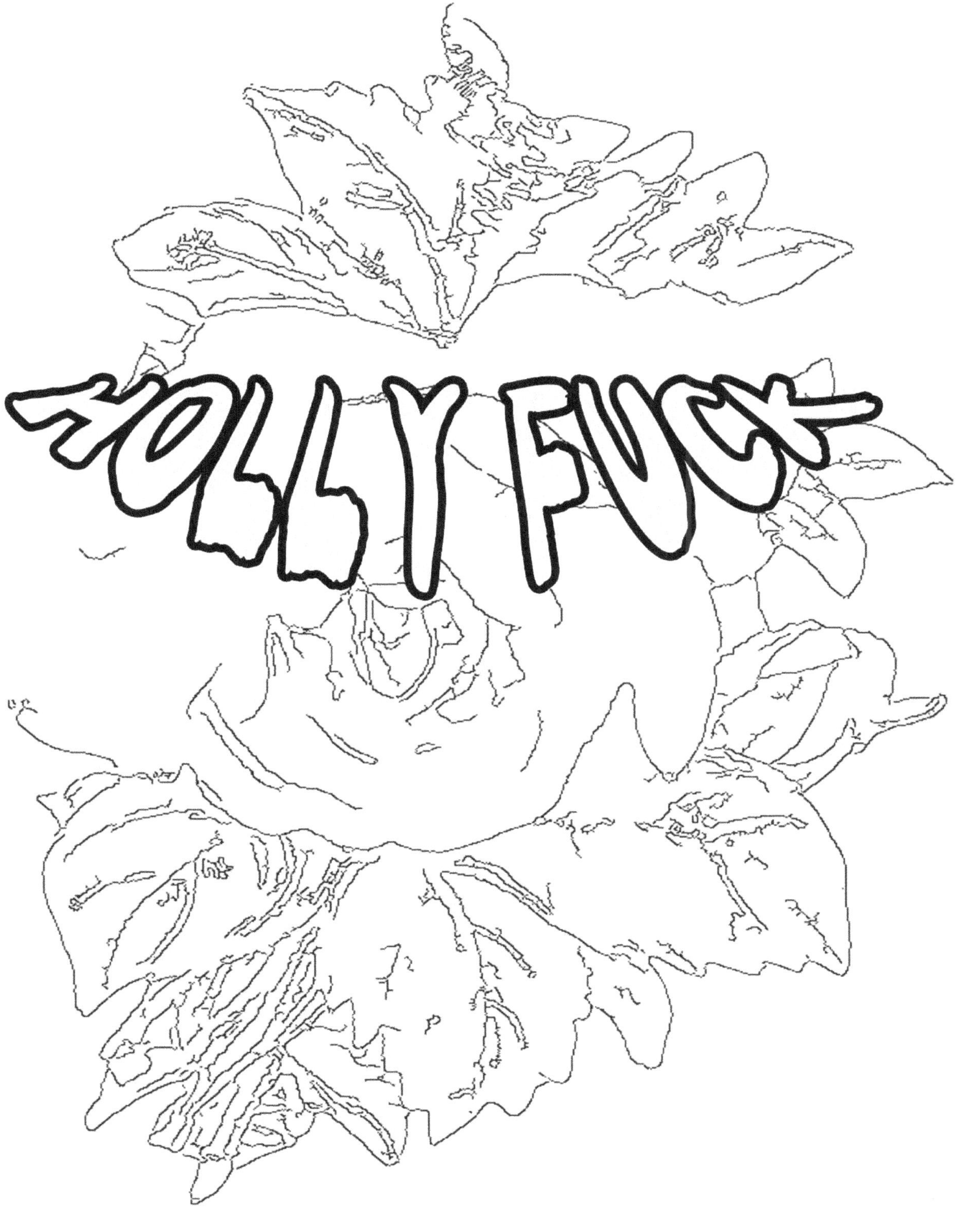
HOLLY FUCK

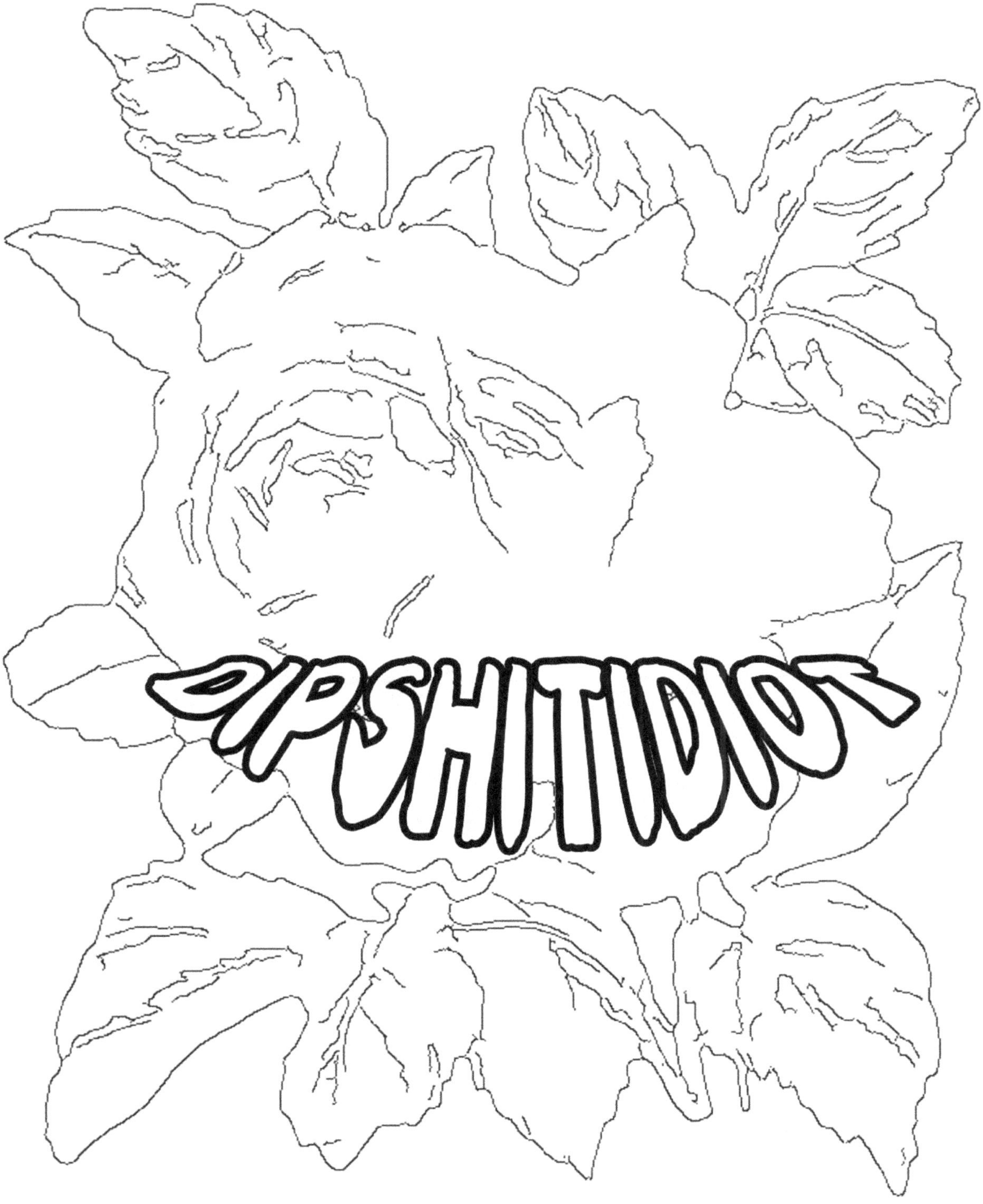
DIPSHITIDIOT

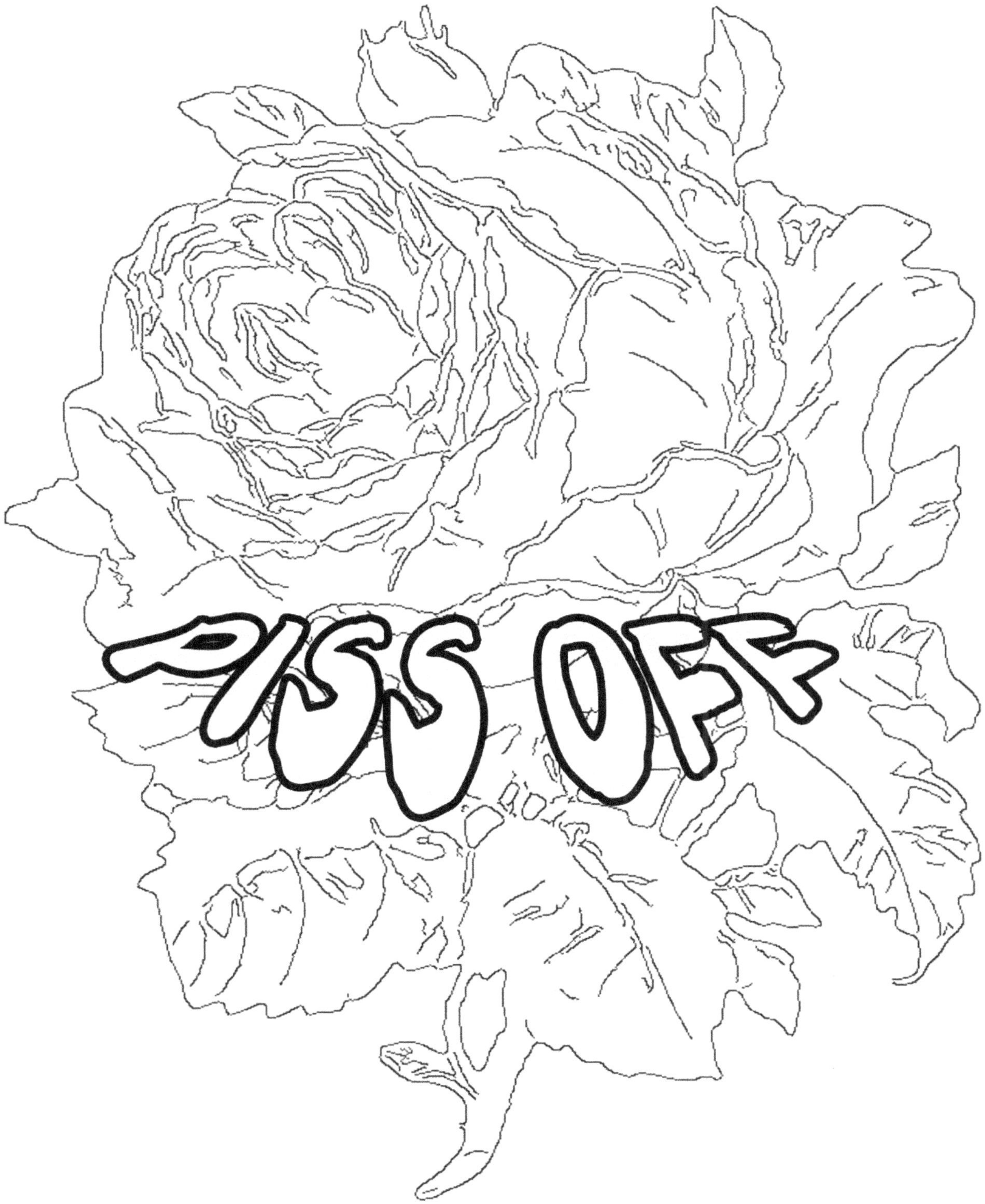
PISS OFF

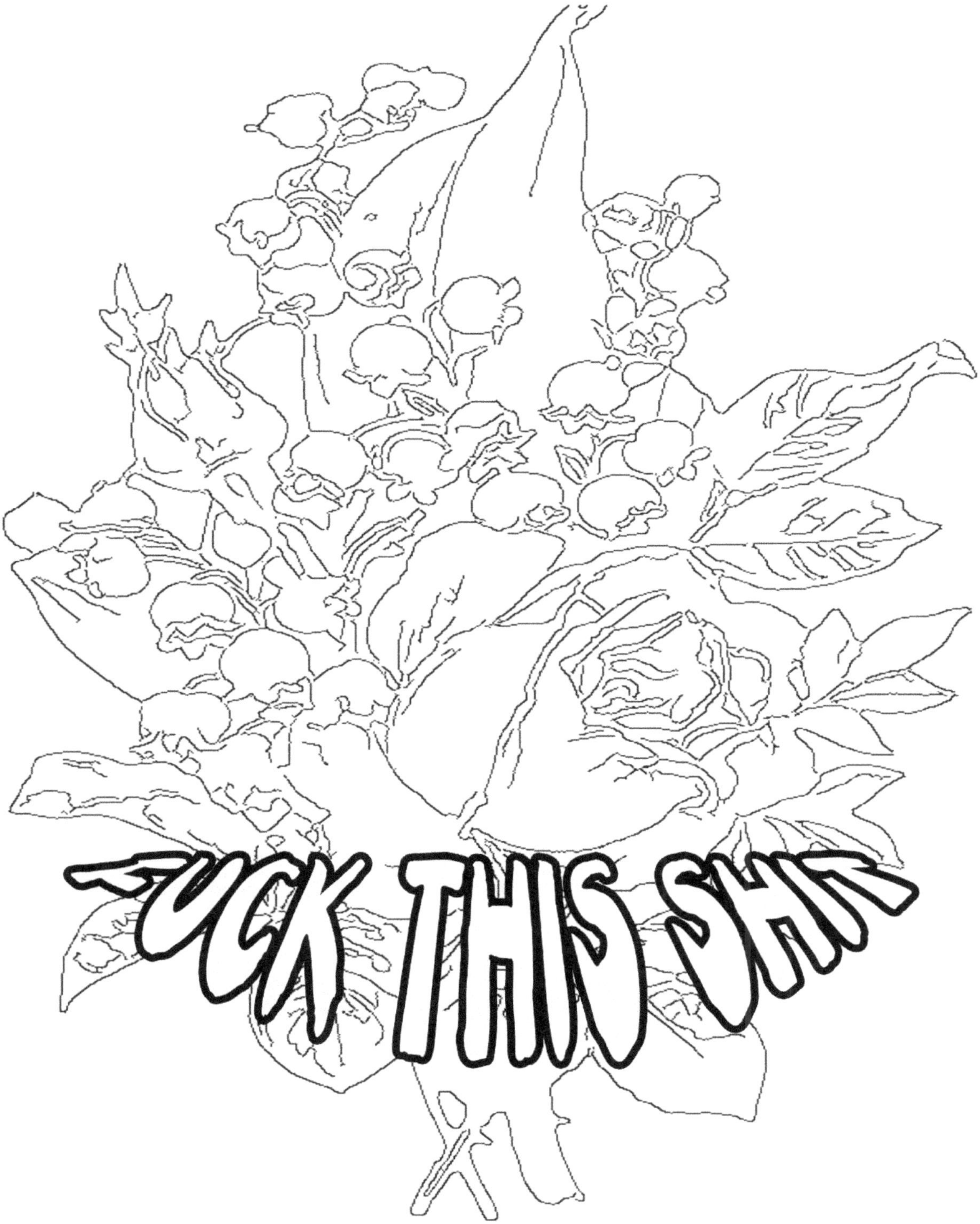
UCK THIS SHI

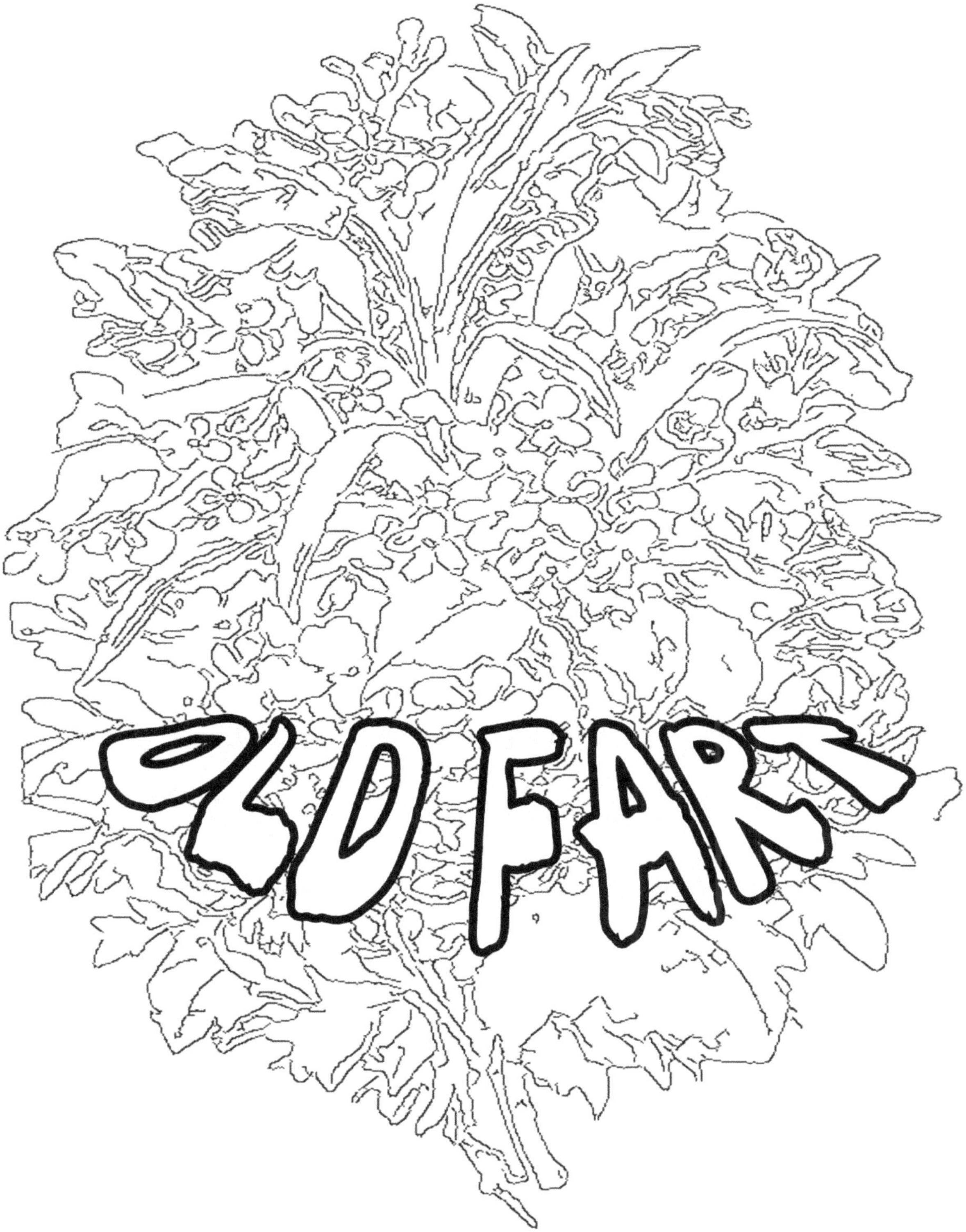
OLD FART

HAVE A GOOD DAY.

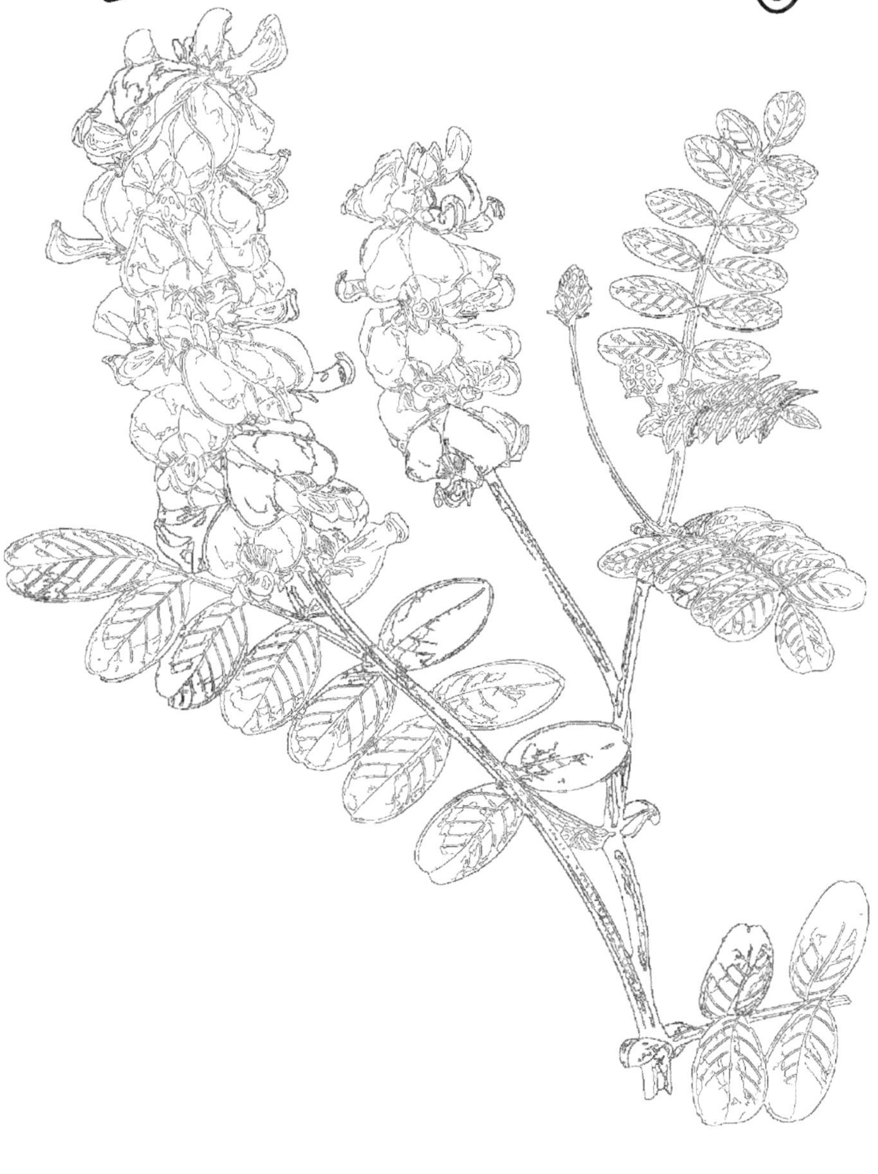

www.ingramcontent.com/pod-product-compliance
Lightning Source LLC
Chambersburg PA
CBHW081620220526
45468CB00010B/2960

* 9 7 8 1 9 8 3 7 3 0 9 6 2 *